PIANO . VOCAL . GUITAR

Disney
ON BROADWAY

ISBN 978-1-4234-5624-7

WALT DISNEY MUSIC COMPANY
WONDERLAND MUSIC COMPANY, INC.

DISTRIBUTED BY

HAL•LEONARD®
CORPORATION

7777 W. Bluemound Rd. P.O. Box 13819 Milwaukee, WI 53213

Visit Hal Leonard Online at
www.halleonard.com

ELABORATE LIVES

from Elton John and Tim Rice's AIDA

Music by ELTON JOHN
Lyrics by TIM RICE

Moderately, with rubato

WRITTEN IN THE STARS

from Elton John and Tim Rice's AIDA

Music by ELTON JOHN
Lyrics by TIM RICE

Moderate Ballad

BE OUR GUEST

from Walt Disney's BEAUTY AND THE BEAST: THE BROADWAY MUSICAL

Lyrics by HOWARD ASHMAN
Music by ALAN MENKEN

LUMIERE: *Ma chère Mademoiselle! It is with deepest pride and greatest pleasure that*

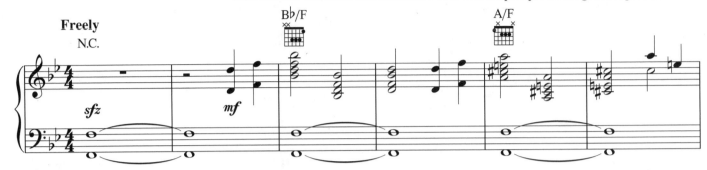

we welcome you here tonight. And now, we invite you to relax. Let us pull up a chair as the dining room proudly presents...

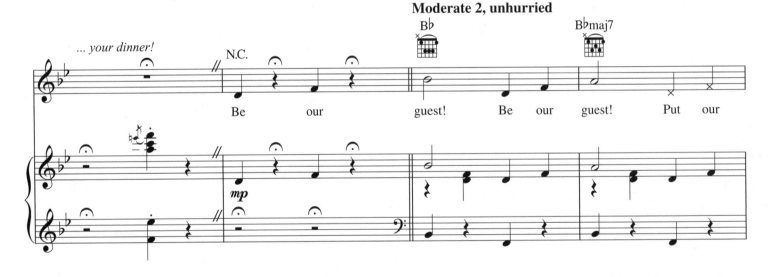

... your dinner!

Be our guest! Be our guest! Put our

ser - vice to the test. Tie your nap - kin 'round your neck, *cher - ie,* and

CHORUS: Be our guest! Be our guest! Get your wor - ries off your

Ah

joyfully

MRS. POTTS: It's a

guest! It's a guest! Sakes a- live, well, I'll be blessed. Wine's been

28

Fast 2, Broadway style

help you. We'll keep go - ing course by

Much slower

course, one by one, 'til you shout: "E-nough! I'm done!" Then we'll

ff *accel. poco a poco*

sing you off to sleep as you di - gest.

A tempo

N.C.

To - night you'll

prop your feet ____ up. But for now, let's eat ____ up. Be our

BEAUTY AND THE BEAST

from Walt Disney's BEAUTY AND THE BEAST: THE BROADWAY MUSICAL

Lyrics by HOWARD ASHMAN
Music by ALAN MENKEN

HUMAN AGAIN

from Walt Disney's BEAUTY AND THE BEAST: THE BROADWAY MUSICAL

Lyrics by HOWARD ASHMAN
Music by ALAN MENKEN

Gentle Parisian waltz

Lumiere: Ah, oui, my friends.

The day we have waited for... may be at hand!

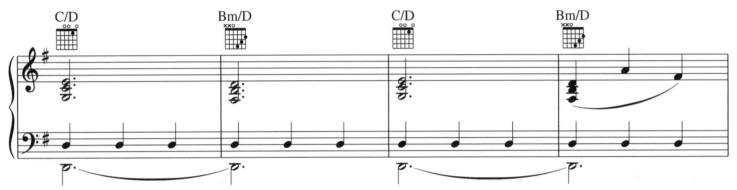

Mrs. Potts: *Oh, if only that were true, Lumiere!*   ***Lumiere:*** *Ah... human again!*

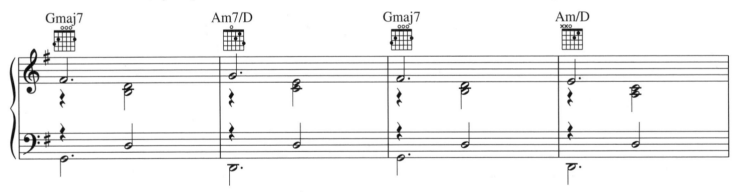

Mrs. Potts: Human again...   ***Lumiere:*** *Yes... think what that means!*   I'll be

48

50

IF I CAN'T LOVE HER

from Walt Disney's BEAUTY AND THE BEAST: THE BROADWAY MUSICAL

Music by ALAN MENKEN
Lyrics by TIM RICE

A CHANGE IN ME

from Walt Disney's BEAUTY AND THE BEAST: THE BROADWAY MUSICAL

Words by TIM RICE
Music by ALAN MENKEN

62

Can You Feel The Love Tonight

from Disney Presents THE LION KING: THE BROADWAY MUSICAL

Music by ELTON JOHN
Lyrics by TIM RICE

SHADOWLAND

from Disney Presents THE LION KING: THE BROADWAY MUSICAL

Music by LEBO M and HANS ZIMMER
Lyrics by MARK MANCINA and LEBO M

Emotionally, slowly

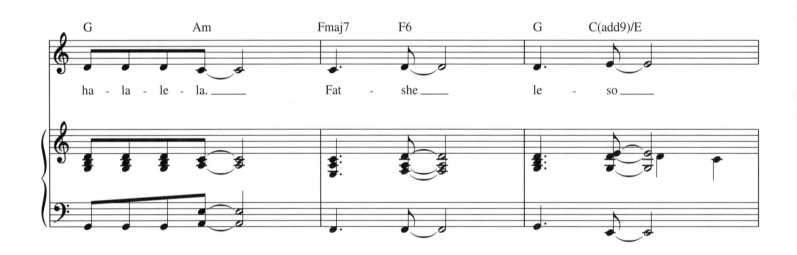

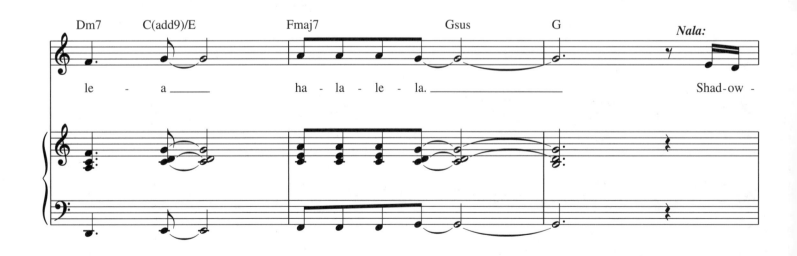

THEY LIVE IN YOU

from Disney Presents THE LION KING: THE BROADWAY MUSICAL

Music and Lyrics by MARK MANCINA,
JAY RIFKIN and LEBO M

Lyrics:

In - gon-ya - ma nengw' en - a - ma-ba - la.

In - gon-ya - ma nengw' en - a - ma-ba - la. Night

and the spir - it __ of life calling.

CIRCLE OF LIFE

from Disney Presents THE LION KING: THE BROADWAY MUSICAL

Music by ELTON JOHN
Lyrics by TIM RICE

I WANT THE GOOD TIMES BACK

from Walt Disney's THE LITTLE MERMAID - A BROADWAY MUSICAL

Music by ALAN MENKEN
Lyrics by GLENN SLATER

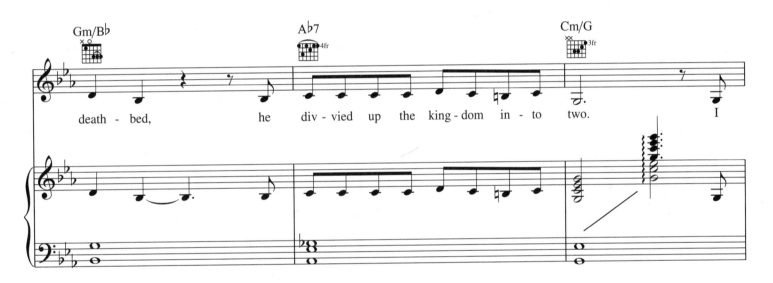

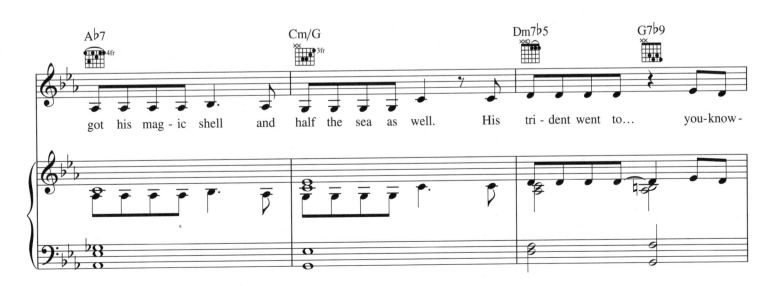

want, just one een-sy, teen-sy thing that I want:

Easy 2

I want the good times back! I want those

grand ol' days! I want the twist-ed nights, the

sick de-lights, the wild soi-rées! I want those

Bbm7 / Db/Eb

all the perks! The tri - dent, crown and throne, all

Eb7 / Gbm6 / Ab7

mine a - lone! The whole damn works! But most of

Db / F7#5 / Bbm

all, I want ol' Tri - ton pinned and wrig - gling on the

Eb9 / F#m7 / F#m6

rack! Then fel - las, it's my time, _____ and frank - ly, it's

BEYOND MY WILDEST DREAMS

from Walt Disney's THE LITTLE MERMAID - A BROADWAY MUSICAL

Music by ALAN MENKEN
Lyrics by GLENN SLATER

With excitement

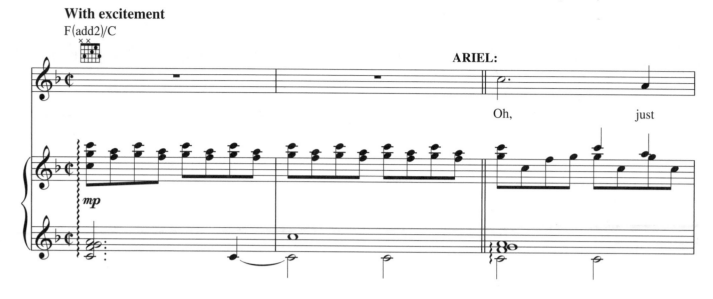

110

ONE STEP CLOSER

from Walt Disney's THE LITTLE MERMAID - A Broadway Musical

Music by ALAN MENKEN
Lyrics by GLENN SLATER

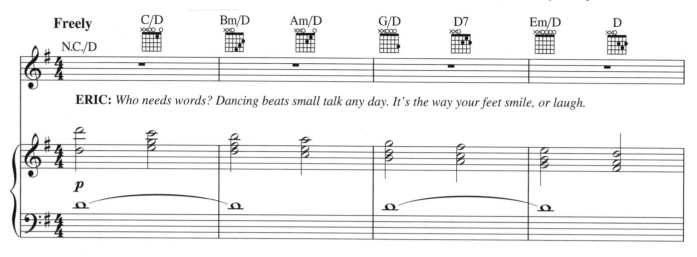

ERIC: *Who needs words? Dancing beats small talk any day. It's the way your feet smile, or laugh.*

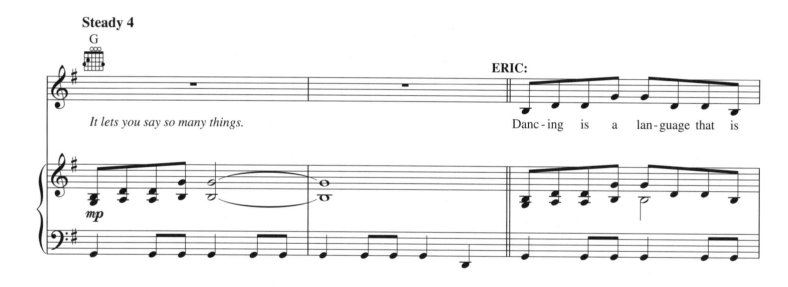

It lets you say so many things.

ERIC: Danc-ing is a lan-guage that is

felt in-stead of heard.

You can

A dance is like a con- ver- sa- tion _____ ex-

cept your lips don't ev- er need to part. And

PART OF YOUR WORLD

from Walt Disney's THE LITTLE MERMAID - A BROADWAY MUSICAL

Music by ALAN MENKEN
Lyrics by HOWARD ASHMAN

ARIEL: *If only I could make my father understand; I just don't see how a world that makes such wonderful things...*

... could be so bad.

ARIEL:
Look at this stuff.

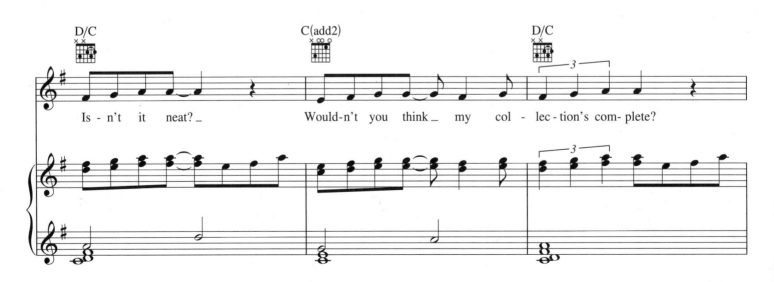

Is-n't it neat? Would-n't you think my col-lec-tion's com-plete?

POSITOOVITY

from Walt Disney's THE LITTLE MERMAID - A BROADWAY MUSICAL

Music by ALAN MENKEN
Lyrics by GLENN SLATER

SCUTTLE: *What's this? You giving up so soon? Ya gotta have a little gumption! A "can-do" kind of attitude!*

Take it from a gull who knows.

SCUTTLE: Now look at me, ya

see this face? In terms of beau-ty, I'm a bas-ket case. And

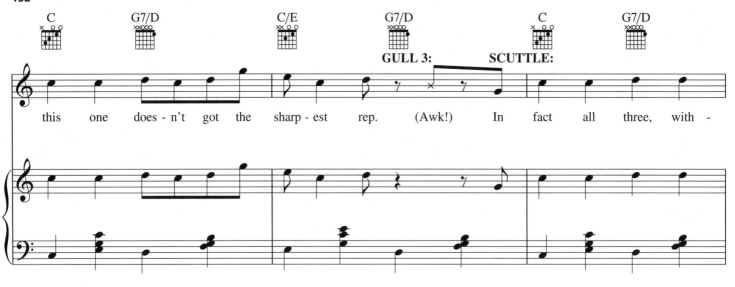

this one does-n't got the sharp-est rep. (Awk!) In fact all three, with-

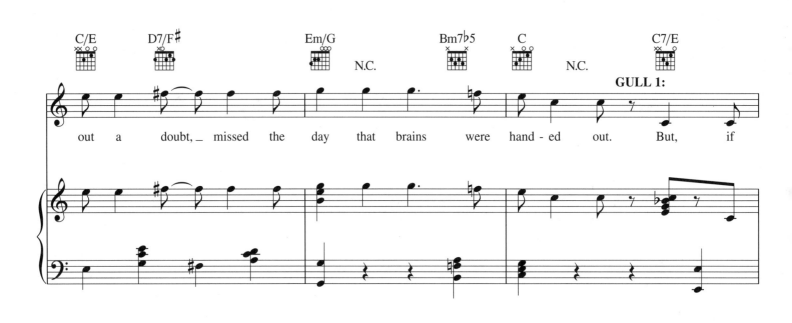

out a doubt,__ missed the day that brains were hand-ed out. But, if

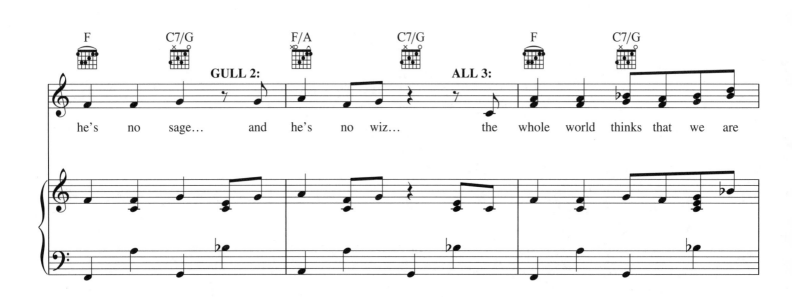

he's no sage... and he's no wiz... the whole world thinks that we are

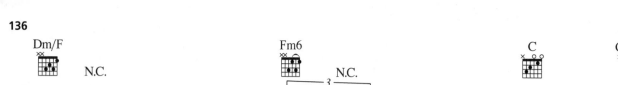

tip is to tap in-to some-thing that you be - lieve. ___

tip is to tap in-to some-thing that you be - lieve. ___

'Cause with the zig and the zug an' the ziz - er - zee, ___ there ain't

Ah ___ ziz - er - zee. ___

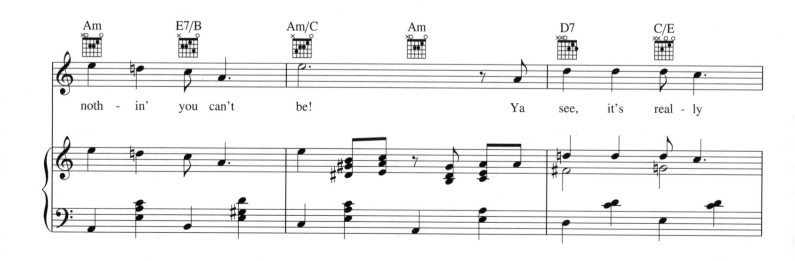

noth - in' you can't be! Ya see, it's real - ly

ANYTHING CAN HAPPEN

from MARY POPPINS

Music by GEORGE STILES
Lyrics by ANTHONY DREWE

PRACTICALLY PERFECT

from MARY POPPINS

Music by GEORGE STILES
Lyrics by ANTHONY DREWE

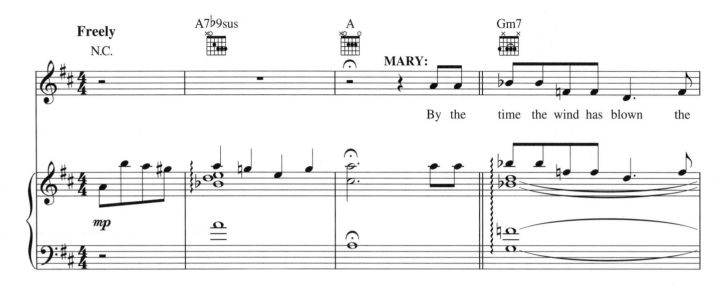

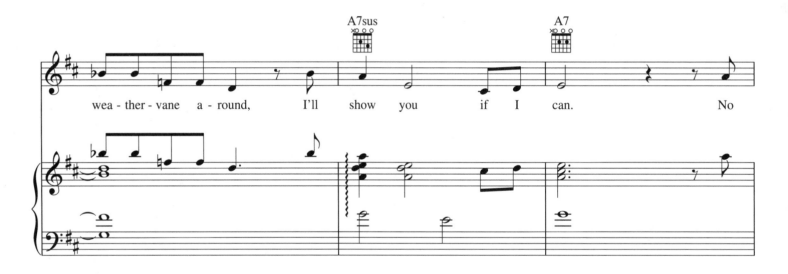

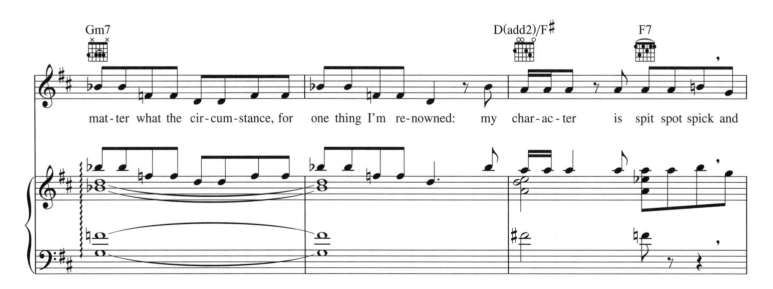

SUPERCALIFRAGILISTIC-EXPIALIDOCIOUS
from the Stageplay MARY POPPINS

Music and Lyrics by RICHARD M. SHERMAN
and ROBERT B. SHERMAN
Additional Music by GEORGE STILES
Additional Lyrics by ANTHONY DREWE

162

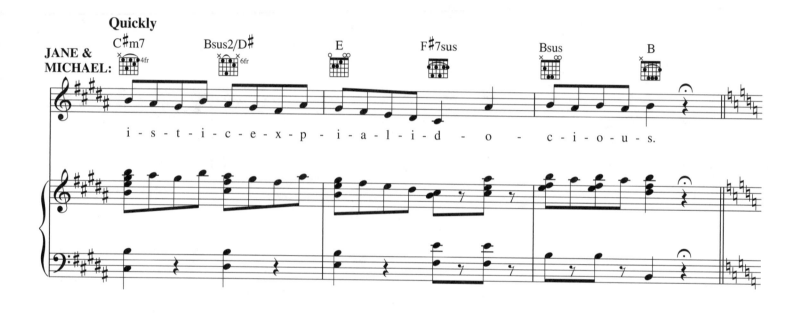

TWO WORLDS

from Disney Presents TARZAN The Broadway Musical

Words and Music by
PHIL COLLINS

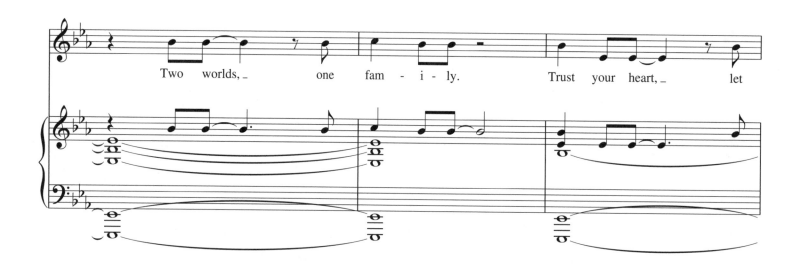

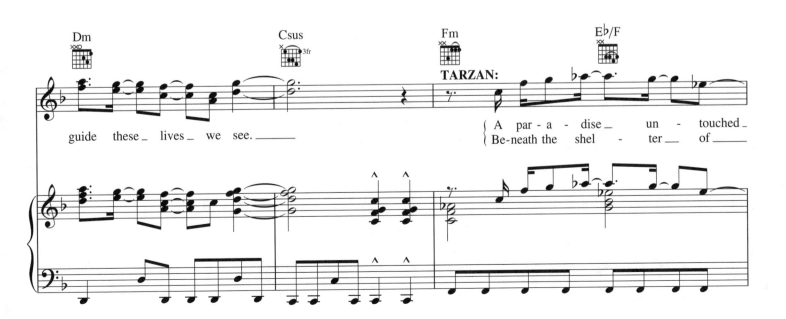

Uptempo Rock

MALE SOLO:

TARZAN:
With ev -'ry end - ing comes a new be - gin - ning. Two worlds, __ one

fam - i - ly. Trust your __ heart, __ let fate de - cide __ to

guide these __ lives, __ to guide these __ lives __ we see. __

TARZAN:

ENSEMBLE:
Put your faith in what you most be - lieve ___ in.

Two worlds, ___ one fam - i - ly!

Two worlds, ___ one fam - i - ly!

YOU'LL BE IN MY HEART

from Disney Presents TARZAN The Broadway Musical

Words and Music by
PHIL COLLINS

DIFFERENT

from Disney Presents TARZAN The Broadway Musical

Music and Lyrics by
PHIL COLLINS

Crisp and steady

TARZAN:

It's just like me, yet it's so dif-fer-ent. Where did it come from? These things it's got here are oh so dif-fer-ent. Where does it be - long?